Dear Parent:
Your child's love of reading starts here!

Every child learns to read in a different way and at his or her own speed. Some go back and forth between reading levels and read favorite books again and again. Others read through each level in order. You can help your young reader improve and become more confident by encouraging his or her own interests and abilities. From books your child reads with you to the first books he or she reads alone, there are I Can Read Books for every stage of reading:

SHARED READING
Basic language, word repetition, and whimsical illustrations, ideal for sharing with your emergent reader

BEGINNING READING
Short sentences, familiar words, and simple concepts for children eager to read on their own

READING WITH HELP
Engaging stories, longer sentences, and language play for developing readers

READING ALONE
Complex plots, challenging vocabulary, and high-interest topics for the independent reader

ADVANCED READING
Short paragraphs, chapters, and exciting themes for the perfect bridge to chapter books

I Can Read Books have introduced children to the joy of reading since 1957. Featuring award-winning authors and illustrators and a fabulous cast of beloved characters, I Can Read Books set the standard for beginning readers.

A lifetime of discovery begins with the magical words **"I Can Read!"**

Visit www.icanread.com for information
on enriching your child's reading experience.

To Tamar
—J.O'C.

For Ted, with appreciation
—R.P.G.

For R.P.G., T.M., J.O'C.
My Flora, Fauna, and
Merryweather for the best
wished-for/wish-granted
gig in the Kingdom.
—T.E.

Many people are allergic to peanuts, and you should always be careful to follow school and classroom policies when using peanut butter.

I Can Read Book® is a trademark of HarperCollins Publishers.

Fancy Nancy: Peanut Butter and Jellyfish Text copyright © 2015 by Jane O'Connor Illustrations copyright © 2015 by Robin Preiss Glasser All rights reserved. Manufactured in China. No part of this book may be used or reproduced in any manner whatsoever without written permission except in the case of brief quotations embodied in critical articles and reviews. For information address HarperCollins Children's Books, a division of HarperCollins Publishers, 195 Broadway, New York, NY 10007. www.icanread.com

Library of Congress catalog card number: 2014937627
ISBN 978-0-06-226976-8 (trade bdg.) — ISBN 978-0-06-226975-1 (pbk.)

14 15 16 17 18   SCP   10 9 8 7 6 5 4 3 2 1   ❖   First Edition

Fancy NANCY

Peanut Butter and Jellyfish

by Jane O'Connor

cover illustration by Robin Preiss Glasser

interior illustrations by Ted Enik

HARPER

An Imprint of HarperCollinsPublishers

Ooh la la!

Our class is at the aquarium.

We will see amazing creatures

that live in the sea.

First we have lunch in the cafeteria.

I open my lunch box.

Inside is a peanut butter
and jelly sandwich,
celery sticks with peanut butter,
and peanut butter cookies.

"The other day,

my dad made peanut butter,"

I tell Clara and Bree.

"He made way too much.

Pretty soon I am going to turn

into a peanut!"

7

Soon it is time to see the exhibits.

We see tropical fish

in every color you can imagine.

We watch sea otters playing
and see a dolphin show.
There is even a pool with manta rays
that we can touch.
(They feel like wet sandpaper!)

Then we come to a special exhibit.

The sign in front says,

"The Wonders of Jellyfish."

"I don't want to go in," I say.

"I detest jellyfish."

(Detest is fancy for hate.)

Once, at the ocean,

I got stung by a jellyfish.

"Don't look at them," Bree tells me.
"Just shut your eyes
and hold on to me."

Bree leads me through the exhibit.

Oops!

I bump into someone.

Oops again!

I bump into someone else.

Then I hear someone say,

"Nancy, is something the matter?"

I open my eyes partway.

It is Ms. Glass.

I explain why I detest jellyfish.

Ms. Glass says, "I understand.

I once got stung by a jellyfish.

But they are amazing sea creatures.

Come look."

Ms. Glass takes my hand.

I cup my hand over my eyes

so I only have to look a little.

We pass by a glass case
of big, blobby, brown jellyfish.
"Ew! Revolting!" I say.
(That means yucky and gross.)
But Ms. Glass keeps insisting that
jellyfish are amazing.

"Jellyfish don't have eyes or ears,"
Ms. Glass says.
"They don't have bones or a heart.
They are made mostly of water.

"The long strings are tentacles.
Those are what sting.
Often jellyfish sting
to defend themselves
against an enemy."

"I was not an enemy!" I tell her.

"I was just swimming

and having fun."

"Yes, but the jellyfish had no way of knowing that," Ms. Glass says. "Jellyfish don't have brains, either."

I guess I see what Ms. Glass means.

The jellyfish wasn't out to get me.

It's not smart enough to do that.

We walk past a case of purple jellyfish.

They aren't as revolting

as the brown jellyfish.

Now we are standing in front of
lots of blue jellyfish.
You can see right through them.
(The fancy word for that
is transparent.)

Then we go stand by another case.

These jellyfish look like

pearly pink bubbles.

In the very last case are tons

of tiny jellyfish with lights.

They blink on and off like fireflies.

I am not so scared anymore.

I guess jellyfish are pretty amazing.

That night,

I tell my family about the aquarium

and the jellyfish.

"I am going to make a diorama

for Ms. Glass because she helped me

overcome my fear."

I explain to JoJo that

a diorama is a 3D display.

I get to work right after dinner.

I find an empty shoe box

and paint the inside blue.

Then I stick long, silvery ribbons

onto one of Mom's old shower caps.

I am making a jellyfish!

Dad helps me hang my jellyfish

from the top of the shoe box.

Then he clears the table.

(No one ate much dinner.

It was chicken

with peanut butter sauce.)

"Too bad I don't have sand

for the bottom," I say.

"Hold on," Dad tells me.

He gets out the giant jar

of homemade peanut butter.

We spoon the last of

the peanut butter

onto the bottom of the shoe box

until the jar is empty.

"It looks exactly like sand,"

I say.

Well, maybe not exactly,

but it's good enough.

I stick seashells

into the peanut butter sand.

Voilà! It looks spectacular.

(That's fancy for great.)

The next morning,

I present the shoe box

to Ms. Glass.

"Oh! A jellyfish diorama!"

she exclaims.

Then I giggle and say,

"No, Ms. Glass.

It's a peanut butter

and jellyfish diorama!"

31

Then I giggle and say,
"No, Ms. Glass.
It's a peanut butter
and jellyfish diorama!"

31

Fancy Nancy's Fancy Words

These are the fancy words in this book:

Detest—hate

Diorama—a 3D display

Revolting—yucky and gross

Spectacular—great

Transparent—see-through